Positive Thinking

A FIVE-MINUTE JOURNAL
TO EMBRACE JOY,
RELEASE NEGATIVITY,
AND LIVE BETTER

PETER PAUPER PRESS, INC.
RYE BROOK, NEW YORK

PETER PAUPER PRESS
Fine Books and Gifts Since 1928

OUR COMPANY

In 1928, at the age of twenty-two, Peter Beilenson began printing books on a small press in the basement of his parents' home in Larchmont, New York. Peter—and later, his wife, Edna—sought to create fine books that sold at "prices even a pauper could afford."

Today, still family owned and operated, Peter Pauper Press continues to honor our founders' legacy—and our customers' expectations—of beauty, quality, and value.

Text by Talia Levy
Cover design by Heather Zschock
Interior design by Keri Steckler
Artwork used under license from Shutterstock.com

Copyright © 2023
Peter Pauper Press, Inc.
3 International Drive
Rye Brook, NY 10573 USA

Published in the United Kingdom and Europe by
Peter Pauper Press, Inc. c/o White Pebble International
Units 2-3, Spring Business Park
Stanbridge Road
Havant, Hampshire PO9 2GJ, UK

Visit us at www.peterpauper.com

Table of Contents

THERE IS JOY AROUND YOU. REACH OUT AND GRASP IT.

Introduction

Wherever you're starting from, this journal will help you forge your own path to greater happiness. You'll dust off your confidence and polish up your inner core of peace. Along the way, you might reconnect with your sense of humor, or let an underappreciated talent shine. You already have the tools you need.

Studies have shown that our brains seek out negative or upsetting things around us, and remember negative experiences more vividly. This inclination can help us recognize danger, or determine that we're in a bad situation. But when we don't need to look sharp for hazards, our problem-seeking survival instinct can suck the joy out of life. It can make us "play it safe" to the point of self-sabotage.

Positive Thinking offers techniques for opening your mind to the good stuff. By adding a five-minute positive thought practice to your day, you'll teach your brain to dwell on good experiences and retain good memories. Over time, you'll form a deeper understanding of what makes you happy, and that understanding will inform your choices.

Read through the pages ahead for a crash course in positive thinking. Then, set aside five minutes each day to fill out a Think Positive Daily Page. YOU'LL BE HAPPY YOU DID.

What Is Positive Thinking?

POSITIVE THINKING IS EXPLORATION. It's the radical act of seeking glimmers of happiness no matter where you are. It's attuning your senses to small pleasures. It's looking at other people with kind eyes, and treating yourself with all the kindness you'd bestow on a dear friend. It's reconnecting with your capacity for surprise and delight.

POSITIVE THINKING IS ABOUT YOUR EXPERIENCE. It might affect what you do, or how people perceive you from the outside, but the real benefit of positivity is inside your own head.

POSITIVE THINKING IS AN END IN ITSELF. The path of positivity may lead you to other life changes, or it may help you derive greater fulfillment from life as it is. Traverse the path for its own sake, with an open mind that's ready to embrace the unexpected.

POSITIVE THINKING STARTS HERE AND NOW. To richly experience good things, we must be present enough to notice them.

POSITIVE THINKING SHAPES YOUR VISION OF YOUR FUTURE. It opens up space for hopes and dreams, bolsters courage, and readies you to embrace positive developments when they happen.

POSITIVE THINKING CAN START ANYWHERE. Maybe life is good generally, and you're trying to reroute some negative thought patterns. Maybe things are really hard right now, and you're looking for a way to sustain your heart. No matter where you are, positivity has something to offer you.

POSITIVE THINKING HAS ROOM FOR *ALL* YOUR EMOTIONS. Even negative ones. You're a human being alive in a complex world that contains causes for fear, anger, and sorrow. It's impossible to avoid these feelings. Sometimes it's natural for grief or anxiety to dominate your emotional landscape, such as after a loss. Positive thinking engages with difficult feelings in ways that lead you toward healing. It quiets impulsivity and illuminates what you need.

POSITIVE THINKING STARTS WITH PAYING ATTENTION TO WHAT YOU FEEL. *Everything* you feel. The more you try to brush off difficult emotions, the more they stick to you like burrs, getting entangled in your life and poking you painfully. Instead of brushing off unpleasant feelings, positive thinking teaches you to look at the feelings closely, name them, and figure out their real causes. It helps you get a little distance from overwhelming emotions, and understand what's going on inside your head.

POSITIVE THINKING IS WHAT YOU NEED IT TO BE. When you begin this journal, do things "by the book" for a while. As you follow the guidance, try the exercises, and journal in the daily pages of this book, you'll notice over time which tools and techniques work best for you. After a month or so, if some practices feel more useful or meaningful than others, try devoting more time to the practices that move you.

Positive and Negative

This book won't teach you to feel only positive emotions or think only positive thoughts. (No book can do that.) Instead, it will help you foster three vital skills:

1. RECOGNIZING AND EXPERIENCING POSITIVE THINGS DEEPLY.

2. FIGURING OUT WHAT YOUR NEGATIVE FEELINGS ARE TELLING YOU, AND WHAT (IF ANYTHING) TO DO ABOUT IT.

3. REFRAMING THE STORIES YOU TELL YOURSELF ABOUT YOUR LIFE.

POSITIVE AND NEGATIVE THOUGHTS AND EXPERIENCES CONTAIN INFORMATION. You can't cut out negative thoughts, and even if you could, you wouldn't want to. Unease may tell us that we need to leave a situation; anger may tell us that something is unjust. Negative feelings are sometimes vital messages about our safety (e.g., "This person is not a safe driver and I shouldn't get in their car") or our mental health (e.g., "This disappointment hit me really hard and I need some time alone to process it").

But positive emotions also offer us key information. If we don't make space for the positive, and give it our time and consideration, we may miss its important messages. A rush of gladness when we see a friend may tell us that their company is good for our mental health, or that we need more social time. A feeling of peace when we step into a forest may indicate that nature benefits our equilibrium.

Being deeply present in good experiences expands our general well-being. It encourages us to flourish, and grants us insight into what flourishing means to us. It helps us find strength and resilience. It solidifies our bonds with the people we care for, and opens us up to new connections. And, critically, connecting with our positive feelings helps us reframe the stories of our lives and experiences in ways that help us grow.

Start with Your Senses

It's easier to try new ways of thinking if you're not totally embroiled in your thoughts. So let's start with a simple, popular technique designed to get you out of your own head. It's a great way to derail a stressful train of thought or to center yourself in the moment, using all five of your senses to bring your present surroundings into focus. Give it a shot!

FIVE FOUR THREE TWO ONE

List **FIVE** things you can **SEE** *(people, cars, plants, animals):*

1. ....

2. ....

3. ....

4. ....

5. ....

List **FOUR** things you can **FEEL OR TOUCH** *(your chair, your clothes, a breeze):*

1. ....

2. ....

3. ....

4. ....

List **THREE** things you can **HEAR** *(conversations, machine sounds, animal sounds):*

1. ....

2. ....

3. ....

List **TWO** things you can **SMELL** *(plants, food, clean laundry):*

1. ....

2. ....

List **ONE** thing you can **TASTE** *(cool air, a snack, lip balm):*

1. ....

Don't worry if you can't come up with enough things for each sense. Just do your best to perceive what's around you.

Try this technique whenever you need to clear your mind. You can write down what you perceive, or just keep track in your head.

A Clear Head

Have you ever done something theoretically enjoyable, but been too distracted to enjoy it? The brain's built-in negative bias can cause stress to color all of our experiences. Stressors saturate our minds, depriving us of the full comfort of a hug, the full taste of a home-cooked meal, the full beauty of a sunset. No matter how pressing a problem is, it doesn't need to occupy our headspace 24/7, and we reap tremendous benefits from a true mental respite.

ON THE NEXT PAGE, LIST SOME THINGS THAT HAVE BEEN WEIGHING ON YOUR MIND. Write until the space is full, or until you run out of things.

THINGS ON MY MIND:

1.

2.

3.

4.

5.

6.

7.

8.

9.

10.

Now, read the first thing you wrote down. Acknowledge it in your mind. Nod to it respectfully, if you like. Then, release it for the moment. It may help to imagine the thought as a bird, which you set free from your cupped hands. DO THE SAME FOR EACH THING ON YOUR LIST.

The problems may still be present, and may still require your attention and effort. Even with unsolved problems on your plate, you can (and deserve to) take mental time away from them. Return to this exercise whenever you have trouble shifting mental gears, or being fully present for the good things in your life.

Three-Minute Meditation

If you meditate, this will sound familiar. If you've never meditated, good news: The exercise requires zero skill, there's no wrong way to do it, and it gets even easier with practice.

For many people, a daily meditation practice increases mental clarity and well-being. Try fitting a regular three-minute meditation into your schedule, and see how it works for you. If this exact meditation method isn't your cup of tea, there are other practices, including alternate breathing techniques, different ways of directing your focus, guided meditations (via an audio track or app), and walking meditation.

READ THE DIRECTIONS BEFORE YOU BEGIN:

1. Sit in a comfortable chair. You can also lie down if that's easier.

2. Set a timer for **3 MINUTES**.

3. Slowly breathe in for a **COUNT OF 6**.

4. Hold your breath for a **COUNT OF 6**.

5. Slowly breathe out for a **COUNT OF 6**.

6. Keep breathing in, holding, and releasing for a **COUNT OF 6** until the timer goes off.

Pay attention to how your breath feels as it flows in and out of your body. Other thoughts will wander into your mind, and that's okay. Acknowledge each thought and release it, just as you did in the previous exercise. It's okay if you have difficulty releasing thoughts, or if many thoughts crowd into your head. Just gently direct your attention back to your breath each time.

Small Joys

GOOD NEWS: For this exercise, you'll need to do something you enjoy. Choose something small that's available where you are now. For example: Make yourself a cup of coffee exactly the way you like it. Pet your dog or cat. Use a soap or lotion that smells good. Open a window and let the breeze waft in.

Spend a few minutes really experiencing the thing you chose. Open your mind to it. What do you see? Feel? Hear? Smell? Taste? (The sharp scent of coffee? The softness of your dog's ears? The rustle of leaves?)

When distracting thoughts arise, acknowledge them and gently redirect your attention to savoring your small joy (taking a sip or bite, holding your cat on your lap, looking at a beautiful image).

When you're done savoring, jot down a few impressions of your small pleasure. What about it was really nice? Did you notice anything that surprised you?

Daily Doses of
GOOD STUFF

Now that you've experimented with deep awareness in the present moment, it's time to expand that awareness.

Name **THREE GOOD THINGS** (big or small) that you experienced in the last day. For example: a loved one's laugh, finding a good seat on the bus, an unexpected compliment, or the first bite of a sandwich when you were really hungry.

1. ....

....

....

....

2. ....

....

....

....

3. ....

....

....

....

Pick one and dwell a little on how it affected you, in the moment or there-after. **DID IT IMPROVE YOUR MOOD?** Make you feel physically better? Reassure you?

NEXT TIME SOMETHING POSITIVE HAPPENS TO YOU, TRY TO SAVOR IT SIMILARLY. Make a note of it on your next daily page in this journal. Over time, you can train your mind to register good experiences as significant and memorable. The good stuff will become a greater part of how you perceive your life.

The Big-Picture Good Stuff

Now, expand your awareness further, encompassing the big picture of your life. **LIST TEN PEOPLE OR THINGS THAT ENRICH YOUR EXISTENCE.** For example: a loved one, a meaningful place, or a passion of yours.

1. _____

2. _____

3. _____

4. _____

5. _____

6. _____

7. _____

8. _____

_____

9. _____

_____

10. _____

_____

CHOOSE ONE ITEM on your list and ruminate on what it means to you. How has it shaped your life? What about it brings you happiness, or facilitates your happiness?

_____

_____

_____

_____

_____

In filling out this journal's daily pages, stay attuned to the big positives in your life. Try to consider them each day with fresh attention and fresh appreciation. You can frame this practice as gratitude, or simply as enhanced awareness of THE GOOD THINGS IN YOUR LIFE.

Decoding Negative Emotions

SO WHAT ABOUT NEGATIVE THOUGHTS AND EMOTIONS?

As mentioned earlier, they're both normal and necessary. Fear, sadness, guilt, and anger are reasonable responses to some of the things the world may throw at you. You can't banish them simply by wishing them away. Sometimes these feelings also contain information that you shouldn't ignore, either about your circumstances or about yourself.

But sometimes emotional distress hits us in disproportion to the situation. In cases like that, we benefit from taking a step back, critically examining what our brains are telling us, and perhaps reframing our narrative.

The trick is figuring out what negative emotions are telling us, when we need to act, and when we need to step back. As you've probably concluded from your own experience, that can be really hard. Some techniques that may help:

START WITH A GROUNDING EXERCISE like "five four three two one" (page 10) or a short meditation (page 14), to get a little distance from the urgency of your feelings.

In writing or in your head, NOTE ONLY THE FACTS OF THE SITUATION. Don't include any speculation, even if it seems obviously true. For example: Let's say you feel awful because you misspoke in conversation, the person you were talking to made a face, and now she must think you're an awkward weirdo. Pare away the speculation, and what you get is: You said something that didn't quite make sense, and her brow furrowed.

ASK YOURSELF: "AM I CATASTROPHIZING?" In the example on the previous page, the person you were talking to might not remember your verbal slip-up at all. If she does, she might not hold it against you. Or you might be right about making a poor impression. But you don't know, and until you have more information, fixating on the worst possibility makes no more sense than fixating on any other possibilities.

ASK YOURSELF: "WHAT ARE THE STAKES?" What is the likely impact of the thing that's upsetting you? If the stakes are low, getting some distance and reframing (see page 24) may be your best next action. If the stakes are higher, consider the next question.

ASK YOURSELF: "WHAT DO I NEED TO DO ABOUT THIS, AND WHEN DO I NEED TO DO IT?" Some stressors require an immediate response, others allow you to sleep on it, and still others require no action from you at all. Figuring out what, if anything, you need to do will help you respond constructively.

ASK YOURSELF: "IS THERE SOMETHING ELSE GOING ON WITH ME?" Does a deeper cause underlie your reaction? Did something bring up a bad memory? Are you under physical or emotional duress? Did you sleep badly last night?

Reframing the
PICTURE

Sometimes it helps to shake up your perspective on a negative situation or experience. Especially when the stakes are lower, reframing can reassure you and guide you toward a constructive course of action. Try it, in writing or in your head:

SUM UP THE SITUATION IN BRIEF, OBJECTIVE TERMS. For example: "Due to a miscommunication, I was late to a big meeting."

DESCRIBE HOW YOU FEEL. For example: "I'm mad and anxious. I think they should have communicated the meeting details more clearly, and I'm worried that my lateness reflected badly on me."

TRY TO IMAGINE OTHER PERSPECTIVES. For example: "The person in charge of scheduling the meeting probably feels guilty about the miscommunication."

BRAINSTORM WAYS TO CREATE A POSITIVE OUTCOME. For example: "There's clearly a flaw in our scheduling system, and maybe we can fix it."

REFRAME THE PICTURE. For example: "A recent miscommunication about an important meeting highlighted a flaw in our scheduling system. It's unfortunate that the miscommunication made me late, but I explained the situation and it's unlikely that anyone will hold it against me. And hopefully now that we know, we can fix the system."

What happened: ....

....

....

How I felt/feel: ....

....

....

Possible other perspectives: ....

....

....

....

Possible constructive actions and positive outcomes: ....

....

....

....

Reframe the picture: ....

....

....

....

Affirmations

An affirmation is a one-line pep talk you give yourself. It's a declaration of your worthiness and your strength. Creating affirmations for yourself builds courage.

Affirmations are short because short statements don't let you hedge. Brevity makes it hard to equivocate or dilute the message.

Phrase your affirmations as "I" statements in the present tense. For example: "I'm a talented athlete." "I'm super organized."

START BY WRITING FIVE AFFIRMATIONS FOR YOUR AREAS OF CONFIDENCE. If your cakes win prizes, write "I'm a great baker." If friends come to you for your wisdom, write "I give good advice."

1.

2.

3.

4.

5.

Here comes the hard part: **WRITE FIVE AFFIRMATIONS FOR YOUR AREAS OF INSECURITY.** If you're nervous in social situations, try "I'm great company and people enjoy spending time with me." If an upcoming task daunts you, counter that feeling with "I am immensely capable, I've done hard things before, and I can do this."

1. ....

....

2. ....

....

3. ....

....

4. ....

....

5. ....

....

Using the Daily Pages

The daily pages are a mini workout for your positive-thinking muscles. Given time, they'll teach your mind to foreground positive experiences and thoughts, balancing your natural human impulse to prioritize the negative.

Each page is designed to be filled out in five minutes or less. The first few may take longer, but once your positivity practice falls into its rhythm, they'll be a breeze.

PARTS OF A DAILY PAGE

DATE AND TIME: Knowing when you filled out each page will make this journal more useful as a record. Experiment with the time of day at which you fill out your daily page. Do you feel energetic and hopeful in the morning, but melancholy at night, or vice versa?

BEST MOOD OF THE LAST DAY: Circle to rate your best mood in the last twenty-four hours. Do you recall anything that prompted it?

NOTABLE EVENTS IN THE LAST DAY: Anything significant that happened.

MAJOR FEELINGS IN THE LAST DAY: Check off all the feelings you recall experiencing in a significant way.

HOW DO YOU FEEL PHYSICALLY? Circle to rate your physical well-being in the last twenty-four hours. Is there anything that needs attention?

THREE GOOD EXPERIENCES IN THE LAST DAY: These can be as small as a tasty snack, or as big as a life event. See page 18 for more ideas and guidance.

ONE MAJOR GOOD THING IN YOUR LIFE: Zoom out and look at the big picture, then make note of something major that's good in your life. It's okay to repeat yourself from day to day. See page 20 for more ideas and guidance.

AFFIRMATION FOR TODAY: Pick an affirmation that resonates with you today. It can be one you've used many times before, or a new one you just wrote. See page 26 for more ideas and guidance.

NOTES: Jot down anything else you find relevant or interesting, or use this space to work out your thoughts.

BEST MOOD IN THE LAST DAY

Why did you feel that way?_____

_____

NOTABLE EVENTS in the last day:

....

....

MAJOR FEELINGS IN THE LAST DAY:

☐ CALM	☐ SAD
☐ ANXIOUS	☐ EMBARRASSED
☐ CHEERFUL	☐ CONFIDENT
☐ GLOOMY	☐ AFFECTIONATE
☐ ENERGETIC	☐ ANGRY
☐ TIRED	☐ ANNOYED
☐ INTERESTED	☐ EXCITED
☐ BORED	☐ AFRAID
☐ INSPIRED	☐ PROUD
☐ BLAH	☐ _____
☐ HAPPY	☐ _____

HOW DO YOU FEEL PHYSICALLY?

Is there anything you need to do about it?

Three **GOOD EXPERIENCES** in the last day:

1.

2.

3.

One **MAJOR GOOD THING** in your life:

AFFIRMATION for today:

Notes:

DATE: TIME:

BEST MOOD IN THE LAST DAY

Why did you feel that way? _____

_____

NOTABLE EVENTS in the last day:

_____

_____

MAJOR FEELINGS IN THE LAST DAY:

☐ CALM   ☐ SAD

☐ ANXIOUS   ☐ EMBARRASSED

☐ CHEERFUL   ☐ CONFIDENT

☐ GLOOMY   ☐ AFFECTIONATE

☐ ENERGETIC   ☐ ANGRY

☐ TIRED   ☐ ANNOYED

☐ INTERESTED   ☐ EXCITED

☐ BORED   ☐ AFRAID

☐ INSPIRED   ☐ PROUD

☐ BLAH   ☐ _____

☐ HAPPY   ☐ _____

HOW DO YOU FEEL PHYSICALLY?

Is there anything you need to do about it?

Three **GOOD EXPERIENCES** in the last day:

1.

2.

3.

One **MAJOR GOOD THING** in your life:

AFFIRMATION for today:

Notes:

DATE: **TIME:**

BEST MOOD IN THE LAST DAY

Why did you feel that way?_____

_____

NOTABLE EVENTS in the last day:

....

....

MAJOR FEELINGS IN THE LAST DAY:

☐ CALM   ☐ SAD

☐ ANXIOUS   ☐ EMBARRASSED

☐ CHEERFUL   ☐ CONFIDENT

☐ GLOOMY   ☐ AFFECTIONATE

☐ ENERGETIC   ☐ ANGRY

☐ TIRED   ☐ ANNOYED

☐ INTERESTED   ☐ EXCITED

☐ BORED   ☐ AFRAID

☐ INSPIRED   ☐ PROUD

☐ BLAH   ☐ _____

☐ HAPPY   ☐ _____

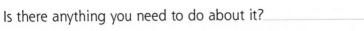
Is there anything you need to do about it?

Three GOOD EXPERIENCES in the last day:

1.

2.

3.

One MAJOR GOOD THING in your life:

AFFIRMATION for today:

Notes:

DATE: **TIME:**

BEST MOOD IN THE LAST DAY

Why did you feel that way? _____

_____

NOTABLE EVENTS in the last day:

....

....

MAJOR FEELINGS IN THE LAST DAY:

☐ CALM   ☐ SAD

☐ ANXIOUS   ☐ EMBARRASSED

☐ CHEERFUL   ☐ CONFIDENT

☐ GLOOMY   ☐ AFFECTIONATE

☐ ENERGETIC   ☐ ANGRY

☐ TIRED   ☐ ANNOYED

☐ INTERESTED   ☐ EXCITED

☐ BORED   ☐ AFRAID

☐ INSPIRED   ☐ PROUD

☐ BLAH   ☐ _____

☐ HAPPY   ☐ _____

Is there anything you need to do about it?

Three **GOOD EXPERIENCES** in the last day:

1.

2.

3.

One **MAJOR GOOD THING** in your life:

AFFIRMATION for today:

Notes:

DATE: **TIME:**

BEST MOOD IN THE LAST DAY

Why did you feel that way? _____

_____

NOTABLE EVENTS in the last day:

....

....

MAJOR FEELINGS IN THE LAST DAY:

☐ CALM	☐ SAD
☐ ANXIOUS	☐ EMBARRASSED
☐ CHEERFUL	☐ CONFIDENT
☐ GLOOMY	☐ AFFECTIONATE
☐ ENERGETIC	☐ ANGRY
☐ TIRED	☐ ANNOYED
☐ INTERESTED	☐ EXCITED
☐ BORED	☐ AFRAID
☐ INSPIRED	☐ PROUD
☐ BLAH	☐ _____
☐ HAPPY	☐ _____

HOW DO YOU FEEL PHYSICALLY?

Is there anything you need to do about it?

Three **GOOD EXPERIENCES** in the last day:

1.

2.

3.

One **MAJOR GOOD THING** in your life:

AFFIRMATION for today:

Notes:

DATE: **TIME:**

BEST MOOD IN THE LAST DAY

Why did you feel that way? _____

_____

NOTABLE EVENTS in the last day:

....

....

MAJOR FEELINGS IN THE LAST DAY:

☐ CALM   ☐ SAD

☐ ANXIOUS   ☐ EMBARRASSED

☐ CHEERFUL   ☐ CONFIDENT

☐ GLOOMY   ☐ AFFECTIONATE

☐ ENERGETIC   ☐ ANGRY

☐ TIRED   ☐ ANNOYED

☐ INTERESTED   ☐ EXCITED

☐ BORED   ☐ AFRAID

☐ INSPIRED   ☐ PROUD

☐ BLAH   ☐ _____

☐ HAPPY   ☐ _____

HOW DO YOU FEEL PHYSICALLY?

Is there anything you need to do about it?

Three GOOD EXPERIENCES in the last day:

1.

2.

3.

One MAJOR GOOD THING in your life:

AFFIRMATION for today:

Notes:

DATE: **TIME:**

BEST MOOD IN THE LAST DAY

Why did you feel that way?_____

_____

NOTABLE EVENTS in the last day:

_____

_____

MAJOR FEELINGS IN THE LAST DAY:

☐ CALM	☐ SAD
☐ ANXIOUS	☐ EMBARRASSED
☐ CHEERFUL	☐ CONFIDENT
☐ GLOOMY	☐ AFFECTIONATE
☐ ENERGETIC	☐ ANGRY
☐ TIRED	☐ ANNOYED
☐ INTERESTED	☐ EXCITED
☐ BORED	☐ AFRAID
☐ INSPIRED	☐ PROUD
☐ BLAH	☐ _____
☐ HAPPY	☐ _____

Is there anything you need to do about it?

Three **GOOD EXPERIENCES** in the last day:

1.

2.

3.

One **MAJOR GOOD THING** in your life:

AFFIRMATION for today:

Notes:

DATE: **TIME:**

BEST MOOD IN THE LAST DAY

Why did you feel that way? _____

_____

NOTABLE EVENTS in the last day:

_____

_____

MAJOR FEELINGS IN THE LAST DAY:

- ☐ CALM
- ☐ ANXIOUS
- ☐ CHEERFUL
- ☐ GLOOMY
- ☐ ENERGETIC
- ☐ TIRED
- ☐ INTERESTED
- ☐ BORED
- ☐ INSPIRED
- ☐ BLAH
- ☐ HAPPY

- ☐ SAD
- ☐ EMBARRASSED
- ☐ CONFIDENT
- ☐ AFFECTIONATE
- ☐ ANGRY
- ☐ ANNOYED
- ☐ EXCITED
- ☐ AFRAID
- ☐ PROUD
- ☐ _____
- ☐ _____

Is there anything you need to do about it?

Three GOOD EXPERIENCES in the last day:

1.

2.

3.

One MAJOR GOOD THING in your life:

AFFIRMATION for today:

Notes:

BEST MOOD IN THE LAST DAY

Why did you feel that way? _____

_____

NOTABLE EVENTS in the last day:

....

....

MAJOR FEELINGS IN THE LAST DAY:

☐ CALM	☐ SAD
☐ ANXIOUS	☐ EMBARRASSED
☐ CHEERFUL	☐ CONFIDENT
☐ GLOOMY	☐ AFFECTIONATE
☐ ENERGETIC	☐ ANGRY
☐ TIRED	☐ ANNOYED
☐ INTERESTED	☐ EXCITED
☐ BORED	☐ AFRAID
☐ INSPIRED	☐ PROUD
☐ BLAH	☐ _____
☐ HAPPY	☐ _____

Is there anything you need to do about it?

Three **GOOD EXPERIENCES** in the last day:

1.

2.

3.

One **MAJOR GOOD THING** in your life:

AFFIRMATION for today:

Notes:

BEST MOOD IN THE LAST DAY

Why did you feel that way?

NOTABLE EVENTS in the last day:

MAJOR FEELINGS IN THE LAST DAY:

☐ CALM   ☐ SAD

☐ ANXIOUS   ☐ EMBARRASSED

☐ CHEERFUL   ☐ CONFIDENT

☐ GLOOMY   ☐ AFFECTIONATE

☐ ENERGETIC   ☐ ANGRY

☐ TIRED   ☐ ANNOYED

☐ INTERESTED   ☐ EXCITED

☐ BORED   ☐ AFRAID

☐ INSPIRED   ☐ PROUD

☐ BLAH   ☐

☐ HAPPY   ☐

HOW DO YOU FEEL PHYSICALLY?

Is there anything you need to do about it?

Three GOOD EXPERIENCES in the last day:

1.

2.

3.

One MAJOR GOOD THING in your life:

AFFIRMATION for today:

Notes:

DATE: **TIME:**

BEST MOOD IN THE LAST DAY

Why did you feel that way?

NOTABLE EVENTS in the last day:

MAJOR FEELINGS IN THE LAST DAY:

☐ CALM   ☐ SAD

☐ ANXIOUS   ☐ EMBARRASSED

☐ CHEERFUL   ☐ CONFIDENT

☐ GLOOMY   ☐ AFFECTIONATE

☐ ENERGETIC   ☐ ANGRY

☐ TIRED   ☐ ANNOYED

☐ INTERESTED   ☐ EXCITED

☐ BORED   ☐ AFRAID

☐ INSPIRED   ☐ PROUD

☐ BLAH   ☐

☐ HAPPY   ☐

HOW DO YOU FEEL PHYSICALLY?

Is there anything you need to do about it?

Three GOOD EXPERIENCES in the last day:

1.

2.

3.

One MAJOR GOOD THING in your life:

AFFIRMATION for today:

Notes:

DATE: **TIME:**

BEST MOOD IN THE LAST DAY

Why did you feel that way?_____

_____

NOTABLE EVENTS in the last day:

....

....

MAJOR FEELINGS IN THE LAST DAY:

☐ CALM ☐ SAD

☐ ANXIOUS ☐ EMBARRASSED

☐ CHEERFUL ☐ CONFIDENT

☐ GLOOMY ☐ AFFECTIONATE

☐ ENERGETIC ☐ ANGRY

☐ TIRED ☐ ANNOYED

☐ INTERESTED ☐ EXCITED

☐ BORED ☐ AFRAID

☐ INSPIRED ☐ PROUD

☐ BLAH ☐ _____

☐ HAPPY ☐ _____

52

HOW DO YOU FEEL PHYSICALLY?

Is there anything you need to do about it?

Three GOOD EXPERIENCES in the last day:

1.

2.

3.

One MAJOR GOOD THING in your life:

AFFIRMATION for today:

Notes:

DATE: **TIME:**

BEST MOOD IN THE LAST DAY

Why did you feel that way?

NOTABLE EVENTS in the last day:

MAJOR FEELINGS IN THE LAST DAY:

- ☐ CALM
- ☐ ANXIOUS
- ☐ CHEERFUL
- ☐ GLOOMY
- ☐ ENERGETIC
- ☐ TIRED
- ☐ INTERESTED
- ☐ BORED
- ☐ INSPIRED
- ☐ BLAH
- ☐ HAPPY

- ☐ SAD
- ☐ EMBARRASSED
- ☐ CONFIDENT
- ☐ AFFECTIONATE
- ☐ ANGRY
- ☐ ANNOYED
- ☐ EXCITED
- ☐ AFRAID
- ☐ PROUD
- ☐ _____
- ☐ _____

Is there anything you need to do about it?

Three GOOD EXPERIENCES in the last day:

1.

2.

3.

One MAJOR GOOD THING in your life:

AFFIRMATION for today:

Notes:

DATE: **TIME:**

BEST MOOD IN THE LAST DAY

Why did you feel that way? _____

_____

NOTABLE EVENTS in the last day:

_____

_____

MAJOR FEELINGS IN THE LAST DAY:

☐ CALM   ☐ SAD

☐ ANXIOUS   ☐ EMBARRASSED

☐ CHEERFUL   ☐ CONFIDENT

☐ GLOOMY   ☐ AFFECTIONATE

☐ ENERGETIC   ☐ ANGRY

☐ TIRED   ☐ ANNOYED

☐ INTERESTED   ☐ EXCITED

☐ BORED   ☐ AFRAID

☐ INSPIRED   ☐ PROUD

☐ BLAH   ☐ _____

☐ HAPPY   ☐ _____

HOW DO YOU FEEL PHYSICALLY?

Is there anything you need to do about it?

Three GOOD EXPERIENCES in the last day:

1.

2.

3.

One MAJOR GOOD THING in your life:

AFFIRMATION for today:

Notes:

DATE: TIME:

BEST MOOD IN THE LAST DAY

Why did you feel that way?

NOTABLE EVENTS in the last day:

MAJOR FEELINGS IN THE LAST DAY:

☐ CALM   ☐ SAD

☐ ANXIOUS   ☐ EMBARRASSED

☐ CHEERFUL   ☐ CONFIDENT

☐ GLOOMY   ☐ AFFECTIONATE

☐ ENERGETIC   ☐ ANGRY

☐ TIRED   ☐ ANNOYED

☐ INTERESTED   ☐ EXCITED

☐ BORED   ☐ AFRAID

☐ INSPIRED   ☐ PROUD

☐ BLAH   ☐

☐ HAPPY   ☐

HOW DO YOU FEEL PHYSICALLY?

Is there anything you need to do about it?

Three **GOOD EXPERIENCES** in the last day:

1.

2.

3.

One **MAJOR GOOD THING** in your life:

AFFIRMATION for today:

Notes:

DATE: **TIME:**

BEST MOOD IN THE LAST DAY

Why did you feel that way? _____

_____

NOTABLE EVENTS in the last day:

_____

_____

MAJOR FEELINGS IN THE LAST DAY:

☐ CALM   ☐ SAD

☐ ANXIOUS   ☐ EMBARRASSED

☐ CHEERFUL   ☐ CONFIDENT

☐ GLOOMY   ☐ AFFECTIONATE

☐ ENERGETIC   ☐ ANGRY

☐ TIRED   ☐ ANNOYED

☐ INTERESTED   ☐ EXCITED

☐ BORED   ☐ AFRAID

☐ INSPIRED   ☐ PROUD

☐ BLAH   ☐ _____

☐ HAPPY   ☐ _____

HOW DO YOU FEEL PHYSICALLY?

Is there anything you need to do about it?

Three **GOOD EXPERIENCES** in the last day:

1.

2.

3.

One **MAJOR GOOD THING** in your life:

AFFIRMATION for today:

Notes:

BEST MOOD IN THE LAST DAY

Why did you feel that way? _____

_____

NOTABLE EVENTS in the last day:

....

....

MAJOR FEELINGS IN THE LAST DAY:

☐ CALM   ☐ SAD

☐ ANXIOUS   ☐ EMBARRASSED

☐ CHEERFUL   ☐ CONFIDENT

☐ GLOOMY   ☐ AFFECTIONATE

☐ ENERGETIC   ☐ ANGRY

☐ TIRED   ☐ ANNOYED

☐ INTERESTED   ☐ EXCITED

☐ BORED   ☐ AFRAID

☐ INSPIRED   ☐ PROUD

☐ BLAH   ☐ _____

☐ HAPPY   ☐ _____

HOW DO YOU FEEL PHYSICALLY?

Is there anything you need to do about it?

Three GOOD EXPERIENCES in the last day:

1.

2.

3.

One MAJOR GOOD THING in your life:

AFFIRMATION for today:

Notes:

DATE: **TIME:**

BEST MOOD IN THE LAST DAY

Why did you feel that way? _____

_____

NOTABLE EVENTS in the last day:

_____

_____

MAJOR FEELINGS IN THE LAST DAY:

☐ CALM   ☐ SAD

☐ ANXIOUS   ☐ EMBARRASSED

☐ CHEERFUL   ☐ CONFIDENT

☐ GLOOMY   ☐ AFFECTIONATE

☐ ENERGETIC   ☐ ANGRY

☐ TIRED   ☐ ANNOYED

☐ INTERESTED   ☐ EXCITED

☐ BORED   ☐ AFRAID

☐ INSPIRED   ☐ PROUD

☐ BLAH   ☐ _____

☐ HAPPY   ☐ _____

HOW DO YOU FEEL PHYSICALLY?

Is there anything you need to do about it?

Three GOOD EXPERIENCES in the last day:

1.

2.

3.

One MAJOR GOOD THING in your life:

AFFIRMATION for today:

Notes:

DATE: **TIME:**

Why did you feel that way?

NOTABLE EVENTS in the last day:

MAJOR FEELINGS IN THE LAST DAY:

☐ CALM   ☐ SAD

☐ ANXIOUS   ☐ EMBARRASSED

☐ CHEERFUL   ☐ CONFIDENT

☐ GLOOMY   ☐ AFFECTIONATE

☐ ENERGETIC   ☐ ANGRY

☐ TIRED   ☐ ANNOYED

☐ INTERESTED   ☐ EXCITED

☐ BORED   ☐ AFRAID

☐ INSPIRED   ☐ PROUD

☐ BLAH   ☐ _____

☐ HAPPY   ☐ _____

HOW DO YOU FEEL PHYSICALLY?

Is there anything you need to do about it?

Three **GOOD EXPERIENCES** in the last day:

1.

2.

3.

One **MAJOR GOOD THING** in your life:

AFFIRMATION for today:

Notes:

DATE: **TIME:**

BEST MOOD IN THE LAST DAY

Why did you feel that way? ....

....

NOTABLE EVENTS in the last day:

....

....

MAJOR FEELINGS IN THE LAST DAY:

- ☐ CALM
- ☐ ANXIOUS
- ☐ CHEERFUL
- ☐ GLOOMY
- ☐ ENERGETIC
- ☐ TIRED
- ☐ INTERESTED
- ☐ BORED
- ☐ INSPIRED
- ☐ BLAH
- ☐ HAPPY

- ☐ SAD
- ☐ EMBARRASSED
- ☐ CONFIDENT
- ☐ AFFECTIONATE
- ☐ ANGRY
- ☐ ANNOYED
- ☐ EXCITED
- ☐ AFRAID
- ☐ PROUD
- ☐ ....
- ☐ ....

HOW DO YOU FEEL PHYSICALLY?

Is there anything you need to do about it?

Three GOOD EXPERIENCES in the last day:

1.

2.

3.

One MAJOR GOOD THING in your life:

AFFIRMATION for today:

Notes:

DATE: **TIME:**

BEST MOOD IN THE LAST DAY

Why did you feel that way?_____

_____

NOTABLE EVENTS in the last day:

_____

_____

MAJOR FEELINGS IN THE LAST DAY:

☐ CALM   ☐ SAD

☐ ANXIOUS   ☐ EMBARRASSED

☐ CHEERFUL   ☐ CONFIDENT

☐ GLOOMY   ☐ AFFECTIONATE

☐ ENERGETIC   ☐ ANGRY

☐ TIRED   ☐ ANNOYED

☐ INTERESTED   ☐ EXCITED

☐ BORED   ☐ AFRAID

☐ INSPIRED   ☐ PROUD

☐ BLAH   ☐ _____

☐ HAPPY   ☐ _____

HOW DO YOU FEEL PHYSICALLY?

Is there anything you need to do about it?

Three GOOD EXPERIENCES in the last day:

1.

2.

3.

One MAJOR GOOD THING in your life:

AFFIRMATION for today:

Notes:

DATE: **TIME:**

BEST MOOD IN THE LAST DAY

Why did you feel that way? ....

....

NOTABLE EVENTS in the last day:

....

....

MAJOR FEELINGS IN THE LAST DAY:

☐ CALM   ☐ SAD

☐ ANXIOUS   ☐ EMBARRASSED

☐ CHEERFUL   ☐ CONFIDENT

☐ GLOOMY   ☐ AFFECTIONATE

☐ ENERGETIC   ☐ ANGRY

☐ TIRED   ☐ ANNOYED

☐ INTERESTED   ☐ EXCITED

☐ BORED   ☐ AFRAID

☐ INSPIRED   ☐ PROUD

☐ BLAH   ☐ ....

☐ HAPPY   ☐ ....

Is there anything you need to do about it?

Three **GOOD EXPERIENCES** in the last day:

1.

2.

3.

One **MAJOR GOOD THING** in your life:

AFFIRMATION for today:

Notes:

DATE: **TIME:**

BEST MOOD IN THE LAST DAY

Why did you feel that way? ....

....

NOTABLE EVENTS in the last day:

....

....

MAJOR FEELINGS IN THE LAST DAY:

☐ CALM   ☐ SAD

☐ ANXIOUS   ☐ EMBARRASSED

☐ CHEERFUL   ☐ CONFIDENT

☐ GLOOMY   ☐ AFFECTIONATE

☐ ENERGETIC   ☐ ANGRY

☐ TIRED   ☐ ANNOYED

☐ INTERESTED   ☐ EXCITED

☐ BORED   ☐ AFRAID

☐ INSPIRED   ☐ PROUD

☐ BLAH   ☐ ....

☐ HAPPY   ☐ ....

HOW DO YOU FEEL PHYSICALLY?

Is there anything you need to do about it?

Three GOOD EXPERIENCES in the last day:

1.

2.

3.

One MAJOR GOOD THING in your life:

AFFIRMATION for today:

Notes:

DATE: **TIME:**

BEST MOOD IN THE LAST DAY

Why did you feel that way?

NOTABLE EVENTS in the last day:

MAJOR FEELINGS IN THE LAST DAY:

☐ CALM	☐ SAD
☐ ANXIOUS	☐ EMBARRASSED
☐ CHEERFUL	☐ CONFIDENT
☐ GLOOMY	☐ AFFECTIONATE
☐ ENERGETIC	☐ ANGRY
☐ TIRED	☐ ANNOYED
☐ INTERESTED	☐ EXCITED
☐ BORED	☐ AFRAID
☐ INSPIRED	☐ PROUD
☐ BLAH	☐
☐ HAPPY	☐

HOW DO YOU FEEL PHYSICALLY?

Is there anything you need to do about it?

Three GOOD EXPERIENCES in the last day:

1.

2.

3.

One MAJOR GOOD THING in your life:

AFFIRMATION for today:

Notes:

DATE: _____   **TIME:** _____

BEST MOOD IN THE LAST DAY

Why did you feel that way? _____

_____

NOTABLE EVENTS in the last day:

_____

_____

MAJOR FEELINGS IN THE LAST DAY:

☐ CALM   ☐ SAD

☐ ANXIOUS   ☐ EMBARRASSED

☐ CHEERFUL   ☐ CONFIDENT

☐ GLOOMY   ☐ AFFECTIONATE

☐ ENERGETIC   ☐ ANGRY

☐ TIRED   ☐ ANNOYED

☐ INTERESTED   ☐ EXCITED

☐ BORED   ☐ AFRAID

☐ INSPIRED   ☐ PROUD

☐ BLAH   ☐ _____

☐ HAPPY   ☐ _____

HOW DO YOU FEEL PHYSICALLY?

Is there anything you need to do about it?

Three GOOD EXPERIENCES in the last day:

1.

2.

3.

One MAJOR GOOD THING in your life:

AFFIRMATION for today:

Notes:

DATE: **TIME:**

BEST MOOD IN THE LAST DAY

Why did you feel that way?_____

_____

NOTABLE EVENTS in the last day:

_____

_____

MAJOR FEELINGS IN THE LAST DAY:

☐ CALM   ☐ SAD

☐ ANXIOUS   ☐ EMBARRASSED

☐ CHEERFUL   ☐ CONFIDENT

☐ GLOOMY   ☐ AFFECTIONATE

☐ ENERGETIC   ☐ ANGRY

☐ TIRED   ☐ ANNOYED

☐ INTERESTED   ☐ EXCITED

☐ BORED   ☐ AFRAID

☐ INSPIRED   ☐ PROUD

☐ BLAH   ☐ _____

☐ HAPPY   ☐ _____

80

HOW DO YOU FEEL PHYSICALLY?

Is there anything you need to do about it?

Three GOOD EXPERIENCES in the last day:

1.

2.

3.

One MAJOR GOOD THING in your life:

AFFIRMATION for today:

Notes:

DATE: TIME:

BEST MOOD IN THE LAST DAY

Why did you feel that way? _____

_____

NOTABLE EVENTS in the last day:

....

....

MAJOR FEELINGS IN THE LAST DAY:

☐ CALM   ☐ SAD

☐ ANXIOUS   ☐ EMBARRASSED

☐ CHEERFUL   ☐ CONFIDENT

☐ GLOOMY   ☐ AFFECTIONATE

☐ ENERGETIC   ☐ ANGRY

☐ TIRED   ☐ ANNOYED

☐ INTERESTED   ☐ EXCITED

☐ BORED   ☐ AFRAID

☐ INSPIRED   ☐ PROUD

☐ BLAH   ☐ _____

☐ HAPPY   ☐ _____

HOW DO YOU FEEL PHYSICALLY?

Is there anything you need to do about it?

Three GOOD EXPERIENCES in the last day:

1.

2.

3.

One MAJOR GOOD THING in your life:

AFFIRMATION for today:

Notes:

BEST MOOD IN THE LAST DAY

Why did you feel that way?_____

_____

NOTABLE EVENTS in the last day:

_____

_____

MAJOR FEELINGS IN THE LAST DAY:

☐ CALM   ☐ SAD

☐ ANXIOUS   ☐ EMBARRASSED

☐ CHEERFUL   ☐ CONFIDENT

☐ GLOOMY   ☐ AFFECTIONATE

☐ ENERGETIC   ☐ ANGRY

☐ TIRED   ☐ ANNOYED

☐ INTERESTED   ☐ EXCITED

☐ BORED   ☐ AFRAID

☐ INSPIRED   ☐ PROUD

☐ BLAH   ☐ _____

☐ HAPPY   ☐ _____

HOW DO YOU FEEL PHYSICALLY?

Is there anything you need to do about it?

Three GOOD EXPERIENCES in the last day:

1.

2.

3.

One MAJOR GOOD THING in your life:

AFFIRMATION for today:

Notes:

DATE: **TIME:**

BEST MOOD IN THE LAST DAY

Why did you feel that way?_____

_____

NOTABLE EVENTS in the last day:

_____

_____

MAJOR FEELINGS IN THE LAST DAY:

☐ CALM   ☐ SAD

☐ ANXIOUS   ☐ EMBARRASSED

☐ CHEERFUL   ☐ CONFIDENT

☐ GLOOMY   ☐ AFFECTIONATE

☐ ENERGETIC   ☐ ANGRY

☐ TIRED   ☐ ANNOYED

☐ INTERESTED   ☐ EXCITED

☐ BORED   ☐ AFRAID

☐ INSPIRED   ☐ PROUD

☐ BLAH   ☐ _____

☐ HAPPY   ☐ _____

HOW DO YOU FEEL PHYSICALLY?

Is there anything you need to do about it?

Three **GOOD EXPERIENCES** in the last day:

1.

2.

3.

One **MAJOR GOOD THING** in your life:

AFFIRMATION for today:

Notes:

DATE: **TIME:**

BEST MOOD IN THE LAST DAY

Why did you feel that way? _____

_____

NOTABLE EVENTS in the last day:

....

....

MAJOR FEELINGS IN THE LAST DAY:

☐ CALM   ☐ SAD

☐ ANXIOUS   ☐ EMBARRASSED

☐ CHEERFUL   ☐ CONFIDENT

☐ GLOOMY   ☐ AFFECTIONATE

☐ ENERGETIC   ☐ ANGRY

☐ TIRED   ☐ ANNOYED

☐ INTERESTED   ☐ EXCITED

☐ BORED   ☐ AFRAID

☐ INSPIRED   ☐ PROUD

☐ BLAH   ☐ _____

☐ HAPPY   ☐ _____

HOW DO YOU FEEL PHYSICALLY?

Is there anything you need to do about it?

Three **GOOD EXPERIENCES** in the last day:

1.

2.

3.

One **MAJOR GOOD THING** in your life:

AFFIRMATION for today:

Notes:

DATE: TIME:

BEST MOOD IN THE LAST DAY

Why did you feel that way? _____

_____

NOTABLE EVENTS in the last day:

_____

_____

MAJOR FEELINGS IN THE LAST DAY:

☐ CALM   ☐ SAD

☐ ANXIOUS   ☐ EMBARRASSED

☐ CHEERFUL   ☐ CONFIDENT

☐ GLOOMY   ☐ AFFECTIONATE

☐ ENERGETIC   ☐ ANGRY

☐ TIRED   ☐ ANNOYED

☐ INTERESTED   ☐ EXCITED

☐ BORED   ☐ AFRAID

☐ INSPIRED   ☐ PROUD

☐ BLAH   ☐ _____

☐ HAPPY   ☐ _____

HOW DO YOU FEEL PHYSICALLY?

Is there anything you need to do about it?

Three GOOD EXPERIENCES in the last day:

1.

2.

3.

One MAJOR GOOD THING in your life:

AFFIRMATION for today:

Notes:

DATE: **TIME:**

BEST MOOD IN THE LAST DAY

Why did you feel that way?

NOTABLE EVENTS in the last day:

MAJOR FEELINGS IN THE LAST DAY:

☐ CALM   ☐ SAD

☐ ANXIOUS   ☐ EMBARRASSED

☐ CHEERFUL   ☐ CONFIDENT

☐ GLOOMY   ☐ AFFECTIONATE

☐ ENERGETIC   ☐ ANGRY

☐ TIRED   ☐ ANNOYED

☐ INTERESTED   ☐ EXCITED

☐ BORED   ☐ AFRAID

☐ INSPIRED   ☐ PROUD

☐ BLAH   ☐ _____

☐ HAPPY   ☐ _____

HOW DO YOU FEEL PHYSICALLY?

Is there anything you need to do about it?

Three GOOD EXPERIENCES in the last day:

1.

2.

3.

One MAJOR GOOD THING in your life:

AFFIRMATION for today:

Notes:

DATE: **TIME:**

BEST MOOD IN THE LAST DAY

Why did you feel that way? _____

_____

NOTABLE EVENTS in the last day:

_____

_____

MAJOR FEELINGS IN THE LAST DAY:

☐ CALM	☐ SAD
☐ ANXIOUS	☐ EMBARRASSED
☐ CHEERFUL	☐ CONFIDENT
☐ GLOOMY	☐ AFFECTIONATE
☐ ENERGETIC	☐ ANGRY
☐ TIRED	☐ ANNOYED
☐ INTERESTED	☐ EXCITED
☐ BORED	☐ AFRAID
☐ INSPIRED	☐ PROUD
☐ BLAH	☐ _____
☐ HAPPY	☐ _____

HOW DO YOU FEEL PHYSICALLY?

Is there anything you need to do about it?

Three **GOOD EXPERIENCES** in the last day:

1.

2.

3.

One **MAJOR GOOD THING** in your life:

AFFIRMATION for today:

Notes:

BEST MOOD IN THE LAST DAY

Why did you feel that way?

NOTABLE EVENTS in the last day:

MAJOR FEELINGS IN THE LAST DAY:

☐ CALM   ☐ SAD

☐ ANXIOUS   ☐ EMBARRASSED

☐ CHEERFUL   ☐ CONFIDENT

☐ GLOOMY   ☐ AFFECTIONATE

☐ ENERGETIC   ☐ ANGRY

☐ TIRED   ☐ ANNOYED

☐ INTERESTED   ☐ EXCITED

☐ BORED   ☐ AFRAID

☐ INSPIRED   ☐ PROUD

☐ BLAH   ☐

☐ HAPPY   ☐

HOW DO YOU FEEL PHYSICALLY?

Is there anything you need to do about it?

Three GOOD EXPERIENCES in the last day:

1.

2.

3.

One MAJOR GOOD THING in your life:

AFFIRMATION for today:

Notes:

DATE: **TIME:**

BEST MOOD IN THE LAST DAY

Why did you feel that way?

NOTABLE EVENTS in the last day:

MAJOR FEELINGS IN THE LAST DAY:

☐ CALM   ☐ SAD

☐ ANXIOUS   ☐ EMBARRASSED

☐ CHEERFUL   ☐ CONFIDENT

☐ GLOOMY   ☐ AFFECTIONATE

☐ ENERGETIC   ☐ ANGRY

☐ TIRED   ☐ ANNOYED

☐ INTERESTED   ☐ EXCITED

☐ BORED   ☐ AFRAID

☐ INSPIRED   ☐ PROUD

☐ BLAH   ☐ _____

☐ HAPPY   ☐ _____

HOW DO YOU FEEL PHYSICALLY?

Is there anything you need to do about it?

Three GOOD EXPERIENCES in the last day:

1.

2.

3.

One MAJOR GOOD THING in your life:

AFFIRMATION for today:

Notes:

DATE: **TIME:**

BEST MOOD IN THE LAST DAY 😄 😊 🙂 🙁 😖

Why did you feel that way?

NOTABLE EVENTS in the last day:

MAJOR FEELINGS IN THE LAST DAY:

☐ CALM   ☐ SAD

☐ ANXIOUS   ☐ EMBARRASSED

☐ CHEERFUL   ☐ CONFIDENT

☐ GLOOMY   ☐ AFFECTIONATE

☐ ENERGETIC   ☐ ANGRY

☐ TIRED   ☐ ANNOYED

☐ INTERESTED   ☐ EXCITED

☐ BORED   ☐ AFRAID

☐ INSPIRED   ☐ PROUD

☐ BLAH   ☐

☐ HAPPY   ☐

HOW DO YOU FEEL PHYSICALLY?

Is there anything you need to do about it?

Three GOOD EXPERIENCES in the last day:

1.

2.

3.

One MAJOR GOOD THING in your life:

AFFIRMATION for today:

Notes:

DATE: **TIME:**

BEST MOOD IN THE LAST DAY

Why did you feel that way? _____

_____

NOTABLE EVENTS in the last day:

_____

_____

MAJOR FEELINGS IN THE LAST DAY:

☐ CALM   ☐ SAD

☐ ANXIOUS   ☐ EMBARRASSED

☐ CHEERFUL   ☐ CONFIDENT

☐ GLOOMY   ☐ AFFECTIONATE

☐ ENERGETIC   ☐ ANGRY

☐ TIRED   ☐ ANNOYED

☐ INTERESTED   ☐ EXCITED

☐ BORED   ☐ AFRAID

☐ INSPIRED   ☐ PROUD

☐ BLAH   ☐ _____

☐ HAPPY   ☐ _____

HOW DO YOU FEEL PHYSICALLY?

Is there anything you need to do about it?

Three GOOD EXPERIENCES in the last day:

1.

2.

3.

One MAJOR GOOD THING in your life:

AFFIRMATION for today:

Notes:

DATE: **TIME:**

BEST MOOD IN THE LAST DAY

Why did you feel that way? _____

_____

NOTABLE EVENTS in the last day:

....

....

MAJOR FEELINGS IN THE LAST DAY:

☐ CALM   ☐ SAD

☐ ANXIOUS   ☐ EMBARRASSED

☐ CHEERFUL   ☐ CONFIDENT

☐ GLOOMY   ☐ AFFECTIONATE

☐ ENERGETIC   ☐ ANGRY

☐ TIRED   ☐ ANNOYED

☐ INTERESTED   ☐ EXCITED

☐ BORED   ☐ AFRAID

☐ INSPIRED   ☐ PROUD

☐ BLAH   ☐ _____

☐ HAPPY   ☐ _____

Is there anything you need to do about it?

Three **GOOD EXPERIENCES** in the last day:

1.

2.

3.

One **MAJOR GOOD THING** in your life:

AFFIRMATION for today:

Notes:

DATE: **TIME:**

BEST MOOD IN THE LAST DAY

Why did you feel that way?_____

_____

NOTABLE EVENTS in the last day:

_____

_____

MAJOR FEELINGS IN THE LAST DAY:

☐ CALM   ☐ SAD

☐ ANXIOUS   ☐ EMBARRASSED

☐ CHEERFUL   ☐ CONFIDENT

☐ GLOOMY   ☐ AFFECTIONATE

☐ ENERGETIC   ☐ ANGRY

☐ TIRED   ☐ ANNOYED

☐ INTERESTED   ☐ EXCITED

☐ BORED   ☐ AFRAID

☐ INSPIRED   ☐ PROUD

☐ BLAH   ☐ _____

☐ HAPPY   ☐ _____

HOW DO YOU FEEL PHYSICALLY?

Is there anything you need to do about it?

Three GOOD EXPERIENCES in the last day:

1.

2.

3.

One MAJOR GOOD THING in your life:

AFFIRMATION for today:

Notes:

DATE: **TIME:**

BEST MOOD IN THE LAST DAY

Why did you feel that way?_____

_____

NOTABLE EVENTS in the last day:

_____

_____

MAJOR FEELINGS IN THE LAST DAY:

☐ CALM   ☐ SAD

☐ ANXIOUS   ☐ EMBARRASSED

☐ CHEERFUL   ☐ CONFIDENT

☐ GLOOMY   ☐ AFFECTIONATE

☐ ENERGETIC   ☐ ANGRY

☐ TIRED   ☐ ANNOYED

☐ INTERESTED   ☐ EXCITED

☐ BORED   ☐ AFRAID

☐ INSPIRED   ☐ PROUD

☐ BLAH   ☐ _____

☐ HAPPY   ☐ _____

HOW DO YOU FEEL PHYSICALLY?

Is there anything you need to do about it?

Three GOOD EXPERIENCES in the last day:

1.

2.

3.

One MAJOR GOOD THING in your life:

AFFIRMATION for today:

Notes:

DATE: **TIME:**

BEST MOOD IN THE LAST DAY

Why did you feel that way?_____

_____

NOTABLE EVENTS in the last day:

_____

_____

MAJOR FEELINGS IN THE LAST DAY:

☐ CALM   ☐ SAD

☐ ANXIOUS   ☐ EMBARRASSED

☐ CHEERFUL   ☐ CONFIDENT

☐ GLOOMY   ☐ AFFECTIONATE

☐ ENERGETIC   ☐ ANGRY

☐ TIRED   ☐ ANNOYED

☐ INTERESTED   ☐ EXCITED

☐ BORED   ☐ AFRAID

☐ INSPIRED   ☐ PROUD

☐ BLAH   ☐ _____

☐ HAPPY   ☐ _____

HOW DO YOU FEEL PHYSICALLY?

Is there anything you need to do about it?

Three GOOD EXPERIENCES in the last day:

1.

2.

3.

One MAJOR GOOD THING in your life:

AFFIRMATION for today:

Notes:

DATE: **TIME:**

BEST MOOD IN THE LAST DAY

Why did you feel that way? _____

_____

NOTABLE EVENTS in the last day:

_____

_____

MAJOR FEELINGS IN THE LAST DAY:

- ☐ CALM
- ☐ ANXIOUS
- ☐ CHEERFUL
- ☐ GLOOMY
- ☐ ENERGETIC
- ☐ TIRED
- ☐ INTERESTED
- ☐ BORED
- ☐ INSPIRED
- ☐ BLAH
- ☐ HAPPY

- ☐ SAD
- ☐ EMBARRASSED
- ☐ CONFIDENT
- ☐ AFFECTIONATE
- ☐ ANGRY
- ☐ ANNOYED
- ☐ EXCITED
- ☐ AFRAID
- ☐ PROUD
- ☐ _____
- ☐ _____

HOW DO YOU FEEL PHYSICALLY?

Is there anything you need to do about it?

Three GOOD EXPERIENCES in the last day:

1.

2.

3.

One MAJOR GOOD THING in your life:

AFFIRMATION for today:

Notes:

DATE: **TIME:**

Why did you feel that way? _____

_____

NOTABLE EVENTS in the last day:

_____

_____

MAJOR FEELINGS IN THE LAST DAY:

☐ CALM	☐ SAD
☐ ANXIOUS	☐ EMBARRASSED
☐ CHEERFUL	☐ CONFIDENT
☐ GLOOMY	☐ AFFECTIONATE
☐ ENERGETIC	☐ ANGRY
☐ TIRED	☐ ANNOYED
☐ INTERESTED	☐ EXCITED
☐ BORED	☐ AFRAID
☐ INSPIRED	☐ PROUD
☐ BLAH	☐ _____
☐ HAPPY	☐ _____

Is there anything you need to do about it?

Three **GOOD EXPERIENCES** in the last day:

1.

2.

3.

One **MAJOR GOOD THING** in your life:

AFFIRMATION for today:

Notes:

DATE: _____   TIME: _____

BEST MOOD IN THE LAST DAY

Why did you feel that way? _____

_____

NOTABLE EVENTS in the last day:

_____

_____

MAJOR FEELINGS IN THE LAST DAY:

☐ CALM   ☐ SAD

☐ ANXIOUS   ☐ EMBARRASSED

☐ CHEERFUL   ☐ CONFIDENT

☐ GLOOMY   ☐ AFFECTIONATE

☐ ENERGETIC   ☐ ANGRY

☐ TIRED   ☐ ANNOYED

☐ INTERESTED   ☐ EXCITED

☐ BORED   ☐ AFRAID

☐ INSPIRED   ☐ PROUD

☐ BLAH   ☐ _____

☐ HAPPY   ☐ _____

Is there anything you need to do about it?

Three GOOD EXPERIENCES in the last day:

1.

2.

3.

One MAJOR GOOD THING in your life:

AFFIRMATION for today:

Notes:

DATE: **TIME:**

BEST MOOD IN THE LAST DAY 😄 🙂 🙂 🙁 😢

Why did you feel that way? _____

_____

NOTABLE EVENTS in the last day:

_____

_____

MAJOR FEELINGS IN THE LAST DAY:

☐ CALM

☐ ANXIOUS

☐ CHEERFUL

☐ GLOOMY

☐ ENERGETIC

☐ TIRED

☐ INTERESTED

☐ BORED

☐ INSPIRED

☐ BLAH

☐ HAPPY

☐ SAD

☐ EMBARRASSED

☐ CONFIDENT

☐ AFFECTIONATE

☐ ANGRY

☐ ANNOYED

☐ EXCITED

☐ AFRAID

☐ PROUD

☐ _____

☐ _____

118

HOW DO YOU FEEL PHYSICALLY?

Is there anything you need to do about it?

Three **GOOD EXPERIENCES** in the last day:

1.

2.

3.

One **MAJOR GOOD THING** in your life:

AFFIRMATION for today:

Notes:

DATE: **TIME:**

BEST MOOD IN THE LAST DAY

Why did you feel that way?

NOTABLE EVENTS in the last day:

MAJOR FEELINGS IN THE LAST DAY:

☐ CALM   ☐ SAD

☐ ANXIOUS   ☐ EMBARRASSED

☐ CHEERFUL   ☐ CONFIDENT

☐ GLOOMY   ☐ AFFECTIONATE

☐ ENERGETIC   ☐ ANGRY

☐ TIRED   ☐ ANNOYED

☐ INTERESTED   ☐ EXCITED

☐ BORED   ☐ AFRAID

☐ INSPIRED   ☐ PROUD

☐ BLAH   ☐

☐ HAPPY   ☐

HOW DO YOU FEEL PHYSICALLY?

Is there anything you need to do about it?

Three **GOOD EXPERIENCES** in the last day:

1.

2.

3.

One **MAJOR GOOD THING** in your life:

AFFIRMATION for today:

Notes:

DATE: **TIME:**

BEST MOOD IN THE LAST DAY

Why did you feel that way?_____

_____

NOTABLE EVENTS in the last day:

_____

_____

MAJOR FEELINGS IN THE LAST DAY:

☐ CALM	☐ SAD
☐ ANXIOUS	☐ EMBARRASSED
☐ CHEERFUL	☐ CONFIDENT
☐ GLOOMY	☐ AFFECTIONATE
☐ ENERGETIC	☐ ANGRY
☐ TIRED	☐ ANNOYED
☐ INTERESTED	☐ EXCITED
☐ BORED	☐ AFRAID
☐ INSPIRED	☐ PROUD
☐ BLAH	☐ _____
☐ HAPPY	☐ _____

HOW DO YOU FEEL PHYSICALLY?

Is there anything you need to do about it?

Three GOOD EXPERIENCES in the last day:

1.

2.

3.

One MAJOR GOOD THING in your life:

AFFIRMATION for today:

Notes:

BEST MOOD IN THE LAST DAY

Why did you feel that way? _____

_____

NOTABLE EVENTS in the last day:

_____

_____

MAJOR FEELINGS IN THE LAST DAY:

☐ CALM   ☐ SAD

☐ ANXIOUS   ☐ EMBARRASSED

☐ CHEERFUL   ☐ CONFIDENT

☐ GLOOMY   ☐ AFFECTIONATE

☐ ENERGETIC   ☐ ANGRY

☐ TIRED   ☐ ANNOYED

☐ INTERESTED   ☐ EXCITED

☐ BORED   ☐ AFRAID

☐ INSPIRED   ☐ PROUD

☐ BLAH   ☐ _____

☐ HAPPY   ☐ _____

HOW DO YOU FEEL PHYSICALLY?

Is there anything you need to do about it?

Three **GOOD EXPERIENCES** in the last day:

1.

2.

3.

One **MAJOR GOOD THING** in your life:

AFFIRMATION for today:

Notes:

BEST MOOD IN THE LAST DAY

Why did you feel that way? _____

_____

NOTABLE EVENTS in the last day:

_____

_____

MAJOR FEELINGS IN THE LAST DAY:

☐ CALM	☐ SAD
☐ ANXIOUS	☐ EMBARRASSED
☐ CHEERFUL	☐ CONFIDENT
☐ GLOOMY	☐ AFFECTIONATE
☐ ENERGETIC	☐ ANGRY
☐ TIRED	☐ ANNOYED
☐ INTERESTED	☐ EXCITED
☐ BORED	☐ AFRAID
☐ INSPIRED	☐ PROUD
☐ BLAH	☐ _____
☐ HAPPY	☐ _____

HOW DO YOU FEEL PHYSICALLY?

Is there anything you need to do about it?

Three **GOOD EXPERIENCES** in the last day:

1.

2.

3.

One **MAJOR GOOD THING** in your life:

AFFIRMATION for today:

Notes:

DATE: TIME:

BEST MOOD IN THE LAST DAY

Why did you feel that way? _____

_____

NOTABLE EVENTS in the last day:

_____

_____

MAJOR FEELINGS IN THE LAST DAY:

☐ CALM   ☐ SAD

☐ ANXIOUS   ☐ EMBARRASSED

☐ CHEERFUL   ☐ CONFIDENT

☐ GLOOMY   ☐ AFFECTIONATE

☐ ENERGETIC   ☐ ANGRY

☐ TIRED   ☐ ANNOYED

☐ INTERESTED   ☐ EXCITED

☐ BORED   ☐ AFRAID

☐ INSPIRED   ☐ PROUD

☐ BLAH   ☐ _____

☐ HAPPY   ☐ _____

HOW DO YOU FEEL PHYSICALLY?

Is there anything you need to do about it?

Three GOOD EXPERIENCES in the last day:

1.

2.

3.

One MAJOR GOOD THING in your life:

AFFIRMATION for today:

Notes:

DATE: TIME:

BEST MOOD IN THE LAST DAY

Why did you feel that way?

NOTABLE EVENTS in the last day:

MAJOR FEELINGS IN THE LAST DAY:

☐ CALM   ☐ SAD

☐ ANXIOUS   ☐ EMBARRASSED

☐ CHEERFUL   ☐ CONFIDENT

☐ GLOOMY   ☐ AFFECTIONATE

☐ ENERGETIC   ☐ ANGRY

☐ TIRED   ☐ ANNOYED

☐ INTERESTED   ☐ EXCITED

☐ BORED   ☐ AFRAID

☐ INSPIRED   ☐ PROUD

☐ BLAH   ☐

☐ HAPPY   ☐

HOW DO YOU FEEL PHYSICALLY?

Is there anything you need to do about it?

Three GOOD EXPERIENCES in the last day:

1.

2.

3.

One MAJOR GOOD THING in your life:

AFFIRMATION for today:

Notes:

DATE: _____   TIME: _____

BEST MOOD IN THE LAST DAY

Why did you feel that way? _____

_____

NOTABLE EVENTS in the last day:

....

....

MAJOR FEELINGS IN THE LAST DAY:

☐ CALM   ☐ SAD

☐ ANXIOUS   ☐ EMBARRASSED

☐ CHEERFUL   ☐ CONFIDENT

☐ GLOOMY   ☐ AFFECTIONATE

☐ ENERGETIC   ☐ ANGRY

☐ TIRED   ☐ ANNOYED

☐ INTERESTED   ☐ EXCITED

☐ BORED   ☐ AFRAID

☐ INSPIRED   ☐ PROUD

☐ BLAH   ☐ _____

☐ HAPPY   ☐ _____

HOW DO YOU FEEL PHYSICALLY?

Is there anything you need to do about it?

Three **GOOD EXPERIENCES** in the last day:

1.

2.

3.

One **MAJOR GOOD THING** in your life:

AFFIRMATION for today:

Notes:

DATE: **TIME:**

BEST MOOD IN THE LAST DAY

Why did you feel that way?_____

_____

NOTABLE EVENTS in the last day:

_____

_____

MAJOR FEELINGS IN THE LAST DAY:

☐ CALM ☐ SAD

☐ ANXIOUS ☐ EMBARRASSED

☐ CHEERFUL ☐ CONFIDENT

☐ GLOOMY ☐ AFFECTIONATE

☐ ENERGETIC ☐ ANGRY

☐ TIRED ☐ ANNOYED

☐ INTERESTED ☐ EXCITED

☐ BORED ☐ AFRAID

☐ INSPIRED ☐ PROUD

☐ BLAH ☐ _____

☐ HAPPY ☐ _____

HOW DO YOU FEEL PHYSICALLY?

Is there anything you need to do about it?

Three GOOD EXPERIENCES in the last day:

1.

2.

3.

One MAJOR GOOD THING in your life:

AFFIRMATION for today:

Notes:

DATE: **TIME:**

BEST MOOD IN THE LAST DAY

Why did you feel that way? _____

_____

NOTABLE EVENTS in the last day:

_____

_____

MAJOR FEELINGS IN THE LAST DAY:

☐ CALM	☐ SAD
☐ ANXIOUS	☐ EMBARRASSED
☐ CHEERFUL	☐ CONFIDENT
☐ GLOOMY	☐ AFFECTIONATE
☐ ENERGETIC	☐ ANGRY
☐ TIRED	☐ ANNOYED
☐ INTERESTED	☐ EXCITED
☐ BORED	☐ AFRAID
☐ INSPIRED	☐ PROUD
☐ BLAH	☐ _____
☐ HAPPY	☐ _____

HOW DO YOU FEEL PHYSICALLY?

Is there anything you need to do about it?_____

_____

Three GOOD EXPERIENCES in the last day:

1. _____

2. _____

3. _____

One MAJOR GOOD THING in your life:

_____

AFFIRMATION for today:

_____

_____

Notes:_____

_____

_____

_____

_____

_____

DATE: **TIME:**

BEST MOOD IN THE LAST DAY

Why did you feel that way? _____

_____

NOTABLE EVENTS in the last day:

_____

_____

MAJOR FEELINGS IN THE LAST DAY:

☐ CALM   ☐ SAD

☐ ANXIOUS   ☐ EMBARRASSED

☐ CHEERFUL   ☐ CONFIDENT

☐ GLOOMY   ☐ AFFECTIONATE

☐ ENERGETIC   ☐ ANGRY

☐ TIRED   ☐ ANNOYED

☐ INTERESTED   ☐ EXCITED

☐ BORED   ☐ AFRAID

☐ INSPIRED   ☐ PROUD

☐ BLAH   ☐ _____

☐ HAPPY   ☐ _____

Is there anything you need to do about it?

Three GOOD EXPERIENCES in the last day:

1.

2.

3.

One MAJOR GOOD THING in your life:

AFFIRMATION for today:

Notes:

DATE: **TIME:**

BEST MOOD IN THE LAST DAY

Why did you feel that way? _____

_____

NOTABLE EVENTS in the last day:

_____

_____

MAJOR FEELINGS IN THE LAST DAY:

☐ CALM   ☐ SAD

☐ ANXIOUS   ☐ EMBARRASSED

☐ CHEERFUL   ☐ CONFIDENT

☐ GLOOMY   ☐ AFFECTIONATE

☐ ENERGETIC   ☐ ANGRY

☐ TIRED   ☐ ANNOYED

☐ INTERESTED   ☐ EXCITED

☐ BORED   ☐ AFRAID

☐ INSPIRED   ☐ PROUD

☐ BLAH   ☐ _____

☐ HAPPY   ☐ _____

HOW DO YOU FEEL PHYSICALLY?

Is there anything you need to do about it?

Three **GOOD EXPERIENCES** in the last day:

1.

2.

3.

One **MAJOR GOOD THING** in your life:

AFFIRMATION for today:

Notes:

DATE: **TIME:**

BEST MOOD IN THE LAST DAY

Why did you feel that way? _____

_____

NOTABLE EVENTS in the last day:

_____

_____

MAJOR FEELINGS IN THE LAST DAY:

☐ CALM   ☐ SAD

☐ ANXIOUS   ☐ EMBARRASSED

☐ CHEERFUL   ☐ CONFIDENT

☐ GLOOMY   ☐ AFFECTIONATE

☐ ENERGETIC   ☐ ANGRY

☐ TIRED   ☐ ANNOYED

☐ INTERESTED   ☐ EXCITED

☐ BORED   ☐ AFRAID

☐ INSPIRED   ☐ PROUD

☐ BLAH   ☐ _____

☐ HAPPY   ☐ _____

HOW DO YOU FEEL PHYSICALLY?

Is there anything you need to do about it?

Three **GOOD EXPERIENCES** in the last day:

1.

2.

3.

One **MAJOR GOOD THING** in your life:

AFFIRMATION for today:

Notes:

BEST MOOD IN THE LAST DAY

Why did you feel that way?_____

_____

NOTABLE EVENTS in the last day:

_____

_____

MAJOR FEELINGS IN THE LAST DAY:

☐ CALM   ☐ SAD

☐ ANXIOUS   ☐ EMBARRASSED

☐ CHEERFUL   ☐ CONFIDENT

☐ GLOOMY   ☐ AFFECTIONATE

☐ ENERGETIC   ☐ ANGRY

☐ TIRED   ☐ ANNOYED

☐ INTERESTED   ☐ EXCITED

☐ BORED   ☐ AFRAID

☐ INSPIRED   ☐ PROUD

☐ BLAH   ☐ _____

☐ HAPPY   ☐ _____

HOW DO YOU FEEL PHYSICALLY?

Is there anything you need to do about it?

Three GOOD EXPERIENCES in the last day:

1.

2.

3.

One MAJOR GOOD THING in your life:

AFFIRMATION for today:

Notes:

DATE: TIME:

BEST MOOD IN THE LAST DAY

Why did you feel that way?_____

_____

NOTABLE EVENTS in the last day:

....

....

MAJOR FEELINGS IN THE LAST DAY:

☐ CALM   ☐ SAD

☐ ANXIOUS   ☐ EMBARRASSED

☐ CHEERFUL   ☐ CONFIDENT

☐ GLOOMY   ☐ AFFECTIONATE

☐ ENERGETIC   ☐ ANGRY

☐ TIRED   ☐ ANNOYED

☐ INTERESTED   ☐ EXCITED

☐ BORED   ☐ AFRAID

☐ INSPIRED   ☐ PROUD

☐ BLAH   ☐ _____

☐ HAPPY   ☐ _____

HOW DO YOU FEEL PHYSICALLY?

Is there anything you need to do about it?

Three **GOOD EXPERIENCES** in the last day:

1.

2.

3.

One **MAJOR GOOD THING** in your life:

AFFIRMATION for today:

Notes:

DATE: **TIME:**

BEST MOOD IN THE LAST DAY

Why did you feel that way?_____

_____

NOTABLE EVENTS in the last day:

_____

_____

MAJOR FEELINGS IN THE LAST DAY:

- ☐ CALM
- ☐ ANXIOUS
- ☐ CHEERFUL
- ☐ GLOOMY
- ☐ ENERGETIC
- ☐ TIRED
- ☐ INTERESTED
- ☐ BORED
- ☐ INSPIRED
- ☐ BLAH
- ☐ HAPPY

- ☐ SAD
- ☐ EMBARRASSED
- ☐ CONFIDENT
- ☐ AFFECTIONATE
- ☐ ANGRY
- ☐ ANNOYED
- ☐ EXCITED
- ☐ AFRAID
- ☐ PROUD
- ☐ _____
- ☐ _____

HOW DO YOU FEEL PHYSICALLY?

Is there anything you need to do about it?

Three GOOD EXPERIENCES in the last day:

1.

2.

3.

One MAJOR GOOD THING in your life:

AFFIRMATION for today:

Notes:

DATE: _____   TIME: _____

BEST MOOD IN THE LAST DAY

Why did you feel that way? _____

_____

NOTABLE EVENTS in the last day:

_____

_____

MAJOR FEELINGS IN THE LAST DAY:

☐ CALM   ☐ SAD

☐ ANXIOUS   ☐ EMBARRASSED

☐ CHEERFUL   ☐ CONFIDENT

☐ GLOOMY   ☐ AFFECTIONATE

☐ ENERGETIC   ☐ ANGRY

☐ TIRED   ☐ ANNOYED

☐ INTERESTED   ☐ EXCITED

☐ BORED   ☐ AFRAID

☐ INSPIRED   ☐ PROUD

☐ BLAH   ☐ _____

☐ HAPPY   ☐ _____

HOW DO YOU FEEL PHYSICALLY?

Is there anything you need to do about it?

Three **GOOD EXPERIENCES** in the last day:

1.

2.

3.

One **MAJOR GOOD THING** in your life:

AFFIRMATION for today:

Notes:

DATE: TIME:

BEST MOOD IN THE LAST DAY

Why did you feel that way?

NOTABLE EVENTS in the last day:

MAJOR FEELINGS IN THE LAST DAY:

☐ CALM   ☐ SAD

☐ ANXIOUS   ☐ EMBARRASSED

☐ CHEERFUL   ☐ CONFIDENT

☐ GLOOMY   ☐ AFFECTIONATE

☐ ENERGETIC   ☐ ANGRY

☐ TIRED   ☐ ANNOYED

☐ INTERESTED   ☐ EXCITED

☐ BORED   ☐ AFRAID

☐ INSPIRED   ☐ PROUD

☐ BLAH   ☐ _____

☐ HAPPY   ☐ _____

Is there anything you need to do about it?

Three **GOOD EXPERIENCES** in the last day:

1.

2.

3.

One **MAJOR GOOD THING** in your life:

AFFIRMATION for today:

Notes:

Four-Month
CHECK-IN

How would you describe your mental state WHEN YOU STARTED THIS JOURNAL?

_____

_____

_____

How would you describe your mental state NOW?

_____

_____

_____

How has your DAILY POSITIVITY PRACTICE affected you?

_____

_____

_____

_____

_____

What did you **ENJOY** about your daily positivity practice?

What did you find **CHALLENGING?**

Did you find the exercises at the beginning of the book useful, and if so, did you **RETURN** to any of them?

What TIME OF DAY did you find best for completing the daily pages?

What things did you notice really affected your MOOD? Were you surprised by any of them?

What (if anything) showed up repeatedly in YOUR LISTS of minor and major good things in your life?

What were some of your favorite **AFFIRMATIONS**?

Do you think you'll keep up your **DAILY** positivity practice?

NOTES

NOTES

NOTES